Books for Kids about Minecraft: An

Unofficial Minecraft Book

Table of Contents

Living in Minecraft...3

The Tale of the Wither and the Ender Dragon 23

The Tale of the Mining King...................................42

Living in Minecraft

Hello, I live in Minecraft. My name is Blocky Blockerson. I don't really know my mother and father because you rarely ever meet family in Minecraft.

However, this is a fun place to live in. You don't need any grown-ups around. I like living on my own.

All day I look after my animals and my home. I have really nice house which I built myself. I can make a lot of things.

I didn't even have to go to school for it. Whatever I need, I can make with the help of my crafting table. It's a really awesome one.

The current place where I am is not where I was born though.

In Minecraft, you can make your own homes and travel anywhere and before I settled down, I wanted to see the wide world around me.

I will admit I was a little scared. It isn't easy just starting off on your own. I can also stay up as late as I want to but it gets pretty scary outside.

I have an awesome diamond sword now but when I didn't have it, I wasn't aware of all the dangers I would face.

At night, the Zombies and skeletons come out to play. The first time I saw them, I wasn't sure what was going on, until one of them bit me.

That hurt a lot. My health started to go down. I ran away as quickly as possible and hid behind a tree. That was a scary night.

Now, I am not as scared. Sure when I see a creeper,

I run like crazy but creepers are scary.

They explode when they see you and it deals a lot of

damage to you. After much travelling, I finally

choose to settle in the Mushroom islands. They're

pretty neat.

You get a lot of Mooshrooms which are cows that give mushroom soup instead of milk when you milk them.

Also you don't run into any mobs and monsters when you are on Mushrooms Island.

I still have to travel elsewhere when I need items like wood, stone and others but that feels like going grocery shopping.

All I do is make a list of things I want and then go out and get them.

But while normal grocery shopping can only take an

hour or more, mine can take a few days. I have to

be very careful not to run into any mobs.

Sometimes, my search for better resources can also take me away from for days as well but with the help of my compass, I can always find my way home.

At home I have loads of crops and animals which rely on me for food and water. Well they don't actually rely on me but I like to think they do. I'm very fond of them.

I have cows, sheep, pigs, a wolf-dog which I tamed, and an ocelot-cat which I also had to tame and even a horse. The horse is extremely useful. I get to saddle it up and travel everywhere on it.

One day, I was exploring my Mushroom Island when I came across a cave in the side of the mountain.

Tempted to explore it, I gathered a couple of supplies I would need.

Some pickaxes, spades, food, torches and a chest. Once everything was packed, I headed down the cave.

The cave was pitch black and I was a little scared of what might be inside it but I started out by lighting a torch and stepping inside.

I reminded myself to be brave. Being brave is what gets you through the day. As I lit my way down, it became apparent that there was something ahead of me. Rounding a corner, I came face to face with some cave spiders.

Cave spiders are dangerous creatures. I don't like

killing so I ran down another tunnel, lighting it up as

I went to discourage them from following me.

When it became apparent that they were no longer

following me, I slowed down and chose another

tunnel to get back to where I was.

Slowly I crept ahead and came face to face with a

zombie. Again I started a mad dash through the

tunnels to get away from it.

really should have brought my sword along with me. I was wondering what I was doing inside the cave when I found it, diamonds and obsidian.

They're both rare materials. Obsidian means you

can travel to the Nether region and I had wanted to

do that for quite some time.

slowly mined out all the ores and kept them in my

chest. I didn't want to lose them. As I headed back, I

realized I was a little lost.

Everything around me looked the same and I had placed too many torches to make a proper route.

In my hustle with the Zombies and the Cave Spiders, I had lost my way.

Rounding another narrow path, I saw a tunnel which gave a glimpse of the sky. I hurried down that tunnel and came up on top of a hill.

I was far away from Mushroom Island and it was dark. As I was turning to go back down the tunnel, I heard a hiss.

There was a Creeper nearby. Sure enough, one came running towards me as I was going inside but it was too late.

The creeper exploded, and I tumbled sideways, away from the tunnel. I got up and looked, I was hurt badly and I needed to get inside the tunnel.

As luck would have it, another Creeper crept out of the bushes and started running and exploded right on top of me.

toppled off the hill and plummeted straight to the ground.

For a while I knew blackness. There was nothing around me and then, I was respawned. I travel now, looking for my Mushroom Island, my farm, my animals, my loot.

I grow tired at times but it really feels like I am not

going to get home. My fighting skills are better. I no

longer hide from my enemies.

The Tale of the Wither and

the Ender Dragon

Once upon a time, there were three dragons in the

Minecraft universe. They were all siblings, hatched

in the same nest but each differed from the other in

different ways.

The Dragon of the Overworld was green in color, with scales that showed a hint of blue at times. In the sunlight, its scales would glow in different shades of green and blue.

She could not breathe fire but she was a water dragon. When angered, she could create floods, rivers and seas or make it rain.

The Dragon of the Nether was red in color with scales that glowed amber. She could breathe fire and has a fiery temper. When hatched, the first thing she had done was breathe fire on the sibling right next to her.

This happened to be the Ender Dragon. The only

male in the batch, the Ender dragon was jet black in

color.

It was rumored that he would have been purple in color, much like the amethyst color of his eyes, except that the Nether dragon had scorched his scales off.

When he grew, his color never changed and he remained black. Of all the other dragons, he was the only one who could do magic. For this reason, the End crystals were particularly useful to him.

The other dragons would often shun the Ender dragon. He was always too serious, too gloomy or was pottering around with his crystals.

The Nether dragon had no patience for him and would often deliberately shun him. The Overworld dragon was friendlier but the Ender dragon scared the wood land creatures which were her friends.

Even the Zombies and Skeletons, who were friends with the Nether Dragon, would tremble when the Ender dragon came near them. Tired and alone, the Ender dragon would often hide in the End.

One day, using his crystals and his magic, he crafted his own friends. He showed them to the Overworld dragon who thought they were very clever.

The Endermen would often be allowed to roam the Overworld as well and the Ender dragon was happy to see them getting along with the other troops.

The Endermen were unusual but they were similar to the Ender dragon. He was happy and he spent many days playing with them.

The Nether dragon noticed the absence of the Ender dragon and decided to check on him. When she saw he was playing with the Endermen, she became envious.

She asked the Ender dragon where they came from and the Ender dragon happily told her. The Nether dragon went back to the Nether but she could not rest.

She wanted something like the Endermen. Having no knowledge of magic, she coerced the Ender dragon to give her some friends as well. Reluctantly, the Ender dragon agreed.

Some days later, he gave her the Ghasts and Blazes and Wither Skeletons. For a few days, the Nether dragon was pleased but she glimpsed the Endermen again and grew envious.

The Ghasts, Blazes and Wither Skeletons seemed stupid to her in comparison to the Endermen. Besides, she had only made them to compete with the zombies, skeletons, bats and other creatures the Overworld dragon played with.

She asked then Ender dragon for more creatures but the Ender dragon refused, he did not have the energy to cast another magic spell and some of this End crystals were getting depleted.

He would need to find more before he cast a spell again. The Nether dragon huffed away in anger. In the Nether, she threw a huge tantrum, breaking the earth, spewing fire and creating huge streams of lava.

Then she decided she was going to make her own creatures. So one day, she stole some zombies, some pigs and went down into the End when the End dragon had gone away to hunt for some crystals.

The old crystals were still in the End though. She

didn't know how to use the crystals but she still

made an attempt.

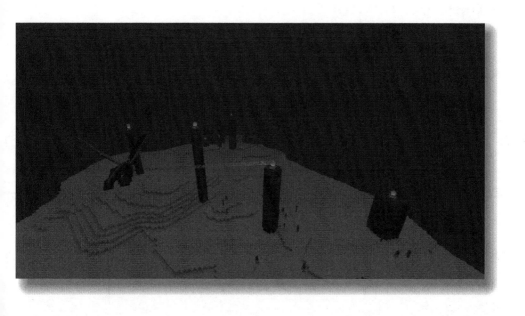

Eventually the crystals began to glow and the whole world shook. Out of the crystals, weird Zombie pigmen started to fall out. The Nether dragon looked on in surprise.

Suddenly, a huge crack split the earth and a Void appeared, it had a huge gravitational pull and the Nether dragon started getting sucked into it.

In a panic, she called for her sister. The Overworld dragon appeared but she was so shocked and stunned that she didn't know what to do.

Not the strongest dragon, she and the Nether dragon got swept into the Void just as the Ender dragon appeared.

The Ender dragon wept for his lost sisters but when he realized what his sister had done, his anger was too great.

He used the crystals to conjure his sisters back but the Void seemed to adverse effect on the magic spells he cast.

Instead of his sisters, a three headed creature slid out of the Void. Panicked and disgusted, the End dragon tried to kill it but it could not die.

As a last resort, the Ender dragon took off the three heads, scattered them in the Nether and crushed his crystals. As long as the Void remained, his magic could not work.

So now, the Ender dragon stays in the End, hoping that one day, his sisters may come back. His spells go awry and often but he still keeps trying.

The Tale of the Mining King

Once upon a time, in Minecraft, there was a miner who loved to mine.

He built himself lovely homes out of all the resources he collected but there was nothing better than digging away in a mine. Hours he spent mining out precious ores.

From emeralds to rubies, to diamonds, gold and silver; it became his passion to collect and use any ore that was in Minecraft.

He knew his father was a miner, much like his grandfather and his grandfather's father. He came from a long line of professional miners.

His other brothers led nomadic lifestyles, much like the NPC villagers. Growing livestock, farming and trading for things they wanted.

They loved the sun, green grass and open plains but he was different. He loved the mountains; he loved caves and most of all he loved spending hours inside the mine hunting for ores.

It was an exhilarating chase to him, to find the ores

hidden beneath the stone, to search for them. He

also loved to smelt and craft new items from them.

Over time, his love for these things made him very

wealthy.

He had a lot of diamonds, gold, silver, jewels and more.

He had built a castle for himself as well and it was magnificent with a gold throne, diamond encrusted walls and rubies, lapis lazuli and other precious ores worked into the decoration as well.

His castle had many different rooms as well but the ones he used and loved the most were the forge, the storage room and the treasury.

In the treasury, he kept all his precious ores, neatly labeled in different chests. The storeroom contained all his tools and the forge was where all the magic happened. Raw ores got smelted into useable materials.

Over time, he made an arrangement with his brothers. He would often trade some items with them in exchange for fuel, tools, food, clothes and other basic items which he either did not have time to make or forgot to make.

Then one day, one of his brothers called him the Mining King as a joke but the others took it seriously. Eventually he was being addressed as the Mining King or the King beneath the Mountain.

Puzzled but not annoyed by it, he let the joke continue because he knew he gave many of the villagers, including his brothers, the precious resources they could not have had without his help.

His prowess in battle was well known as well. No creepers or zombies could attack his castle.

They were long dead, through his traps, before he even got to know about them.

His armor and weapons were made completely from diamond. He had the whole set completed by his third day, a feat which was unheard of.

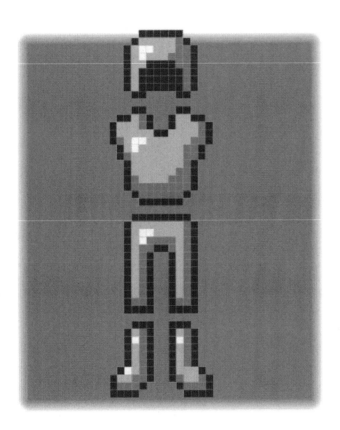

One day, his brothers presented him with a crown they had crafted.

"Brother, it is time to take your seat and assign someone else to do your work."

When he tried to protest, his brothers would not hear of it.

"You are a king; it is not nice to see our king shoveling dirt. Tell us what needs to be done; we will do it for you."

Reluctantly, he handed his pickaxe to the other miners. He directed their work and told them what to do. He was a clever miner and clever as a king as well.

Eventually, he had a team of miners mining for ores. He had a team of smelters, crafters and even a team of farmers.

His brilliant mind helped in planning farming and breeding as well and he soon had the little kingdom flourishing.

There were more than enough resources for everyone to have and share. Yet, the Mining King soon grew bored. All he did everyday was sit on his throne and listen to other people making requests for this or that.

If he wanted anything, there were crafters, smelters, farmers, breeders and miners there to provide him with anything he wanted. He often went on long walks but they bored him.

The land around him was safe. His traps and the warriors he had stationed ensured that there were no harmful mobs around. When he went down to the mines, he would get ushered out by the miners.

"It is not safe, your Majesty." or "Your robes will get dirty, your Highness." And he would be escorted out.

As the wealth, peace and prosperity of the kingdom grew; his brothers started to become envious and plotted against him.

They started making plans to kill him and take his crown. The Mining King's faithful followers overheard and let him know what the brothers were planning.

The Mining King became extremely miserable. As each day passed, his misery grew. All he wanted was to hold a pickaxe, mine for an ore and fight a surprise Cave Spider or a Zombie or two.

He never wanted to fight with his brothers. He wondered what he would do, until he had a brilliant plan. One night, he took of his fine clothes and packed them. He got on some plain clothes and crept down to the treasury.

From each chest, he took five precious ores for himself. Then he went to the forge, he gathered his armor, his favorite pickaxe and his sword.

The last thing he did was grab some food and other basic supplies.

n the middle of the night, he slipped out of the

castle. It saddened him to leave the place but his

happiness at being free was worth it.

He walked away from his castle and his Kingdom and never returned. His brothers never bothered to search for him. Before long, they started fighting amongst themselves for his Kingdom.

Years later, a scruffy stranger came where the ruined castle stood. He appeared confused and asked the few remaining villagers about what happened.

The villagers told him the story of the Mining King, how he disappeared one night and how the Kingdom got tossed around from one brother to another who only did more damage than good.

All agreed that no one ruled it better or kept it better than the Mining King who Disappeared. Many people missed him because of the prosperity and safety he had brought to the Kingdom.

The Kingdom was poor now. The last brother who ruled the castle had just left one day ago with the last of the resources.

Many villagers had abandoned the village until only a handful remained. The only remaining villagers had stayed in the hopes that their Mining King would come back.

That was when the stranger smiled. He opened his chest and showed them the crown. The very same crown his followers had crafted for him.

'Your Mining King has come home,' he said with a warm smile as he placed the crown on his head again. As the people gaped at him, he opened the chest he was carrying and showed them so many ores, some smelted some raw.

His faithful cheered for him and led him inside. With them by his side, the Mining King restored his castle and brought peace and prosperity to his Kingdom again. Of his brothers, no one heard, nor cared to search for.

And they lived happily ever after.